Simple Maths

Adding and Counting On

Richard Leffingwell

www.raintreepublishers.co.uk

Visit our website to find out more information about **Raintree** books.

To order:
- ☎ Phone 44 (0) 1865 888112
- 📄 Send a fax to 44 (0) 1865 314091
- 💻 Visit the Raintree Bookshop at **www.raintreepublishers.co.uk** to browse our catalogue and order online.

First published in Great Britain by Raintree,
Halley Court, Jordan Hill, Oxford OX2 8EJ,
part of Harcourt Education.
Raintree is a registered trademark of
Harcourt Education Ltd.

Editorial: Diyan Leake and Cassie Mayer
Design: Joanna Hinton-Malivoire and
   The Partnership
Picture Research: Erica Newbery
Production: Duncan Gilbert

Originated by Modern Age
Printed and bound in China by
   South China Printing Company

10 digit ISBN 1 4062 0390 4
13 digit ISBN 978 1 4062 0390 5

10 09
10 9 8 7 6 5 4 3 2

British Library Cataloguing in Publication Data
Leffingwell, Richard
Adding and Counting On
513.2'11
A full catalogue record for this book is available
from the British Library.

Acknowledgements

The publishers would like to thank the following
for permission to reproduce photographs: Getty
Images (Photodisc Red/Davies & Starr) p. **22**;
Harcourt Education Ltd (www.mmstudios.co.uk)
pp. **4–21**, back cover

Cover photograph reproduced with permission of
Harcourt Education Ltd (www.mmstudios.co.uk).

The publishers would like to thank Patti Barber,
Specialist in Early Childhood and Primary
Education, Institute of Education, University of
London, for her assistance in the preparation of
this book.

Every effort has been made to contact copyright
holders of any material reproduced in this book.
Any omissions will be rectified in subsequent
printings if notice is given to the publishers.

The paper used to print this book comes from
sustainable resources.

Contents

What is adding?

When you group things together, you are adding them.

Adding helps you find out how many things you have.

Pretend you have 5 toy cars.

Someone gives you 2 more.

Put all the cars together and count them.

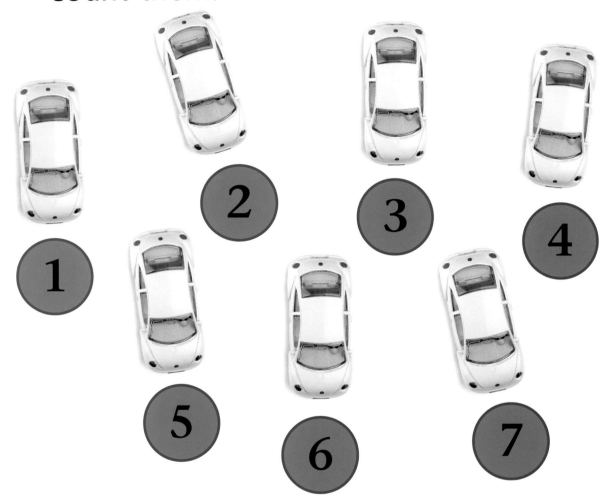

How many do you have?

$$5 + 2 = ?$$

You have 7 cars.

5 + 2 = 7

Adding crayons

4 + 2 = ?

You have 4 crayons and get 2 more.

How many do you have when you add them together?

Count the crayons one by one.

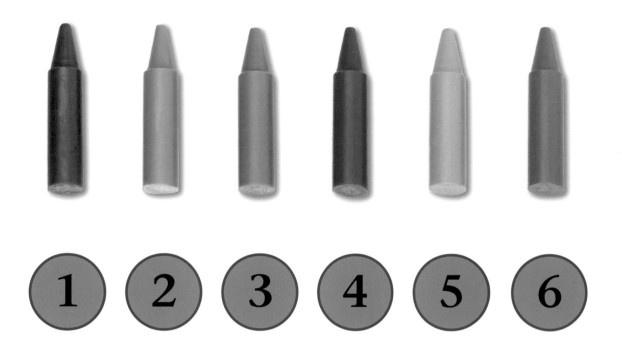

Counting everything takes a long time.

Can you think of another way to find out how many you have?

$$4 + 2 = ?$$

You started with 4 crayons.

You added 2 more.

Start at 4 and count on 2 times.

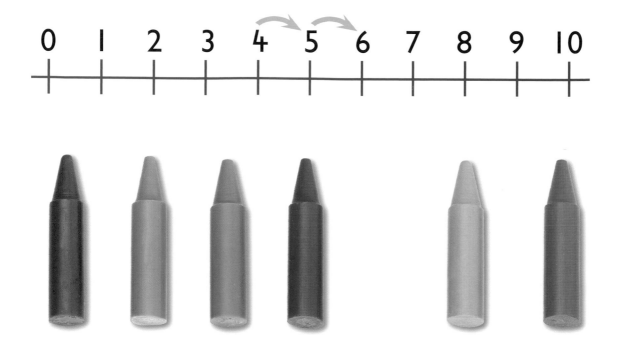

$$4 + 2 = 6$$

Starting with what you have and counting the new items is called counting on.

Adding erasers

$$5 + 3 = ?$$

You have 5 erasers and find 3 more.

Count them all to find out how many you have.

0 1 2 3 4 5 6 7 8 9 10

Now try counting on to find out how many you have.

$$5 + 3 = ?$$

Start with 5 erasers.

Then count on 3 times.

0 1 2 3 4 5 6 7 8 9 10

$$5 + 3 = 8$$

You have **8** erasers.

You can count them all or count on to find the answer.

Counting on is much quicker than counting them all!

Adding balls

You have 6 balls and someone gives you 4 more.

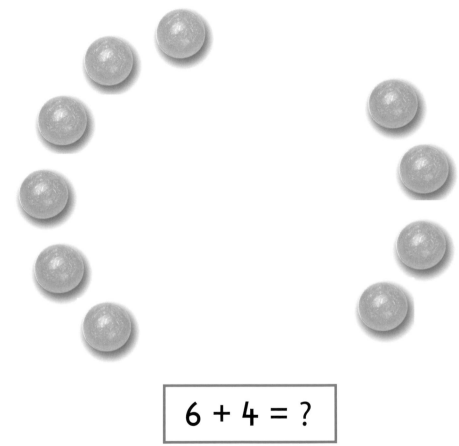

6 + 4 = ?

Count on to find out how many you have.

Start with 6 and count on 4 times.

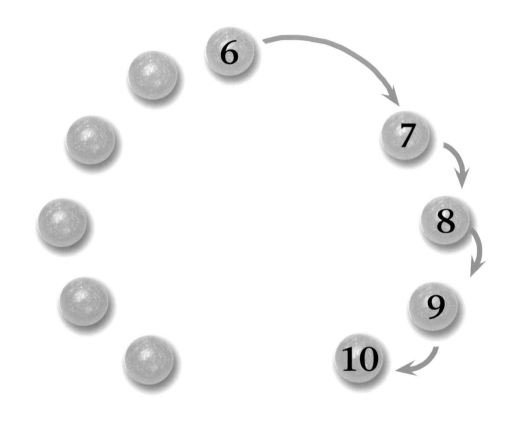

6 + 4 = 10

You have 10 balls.

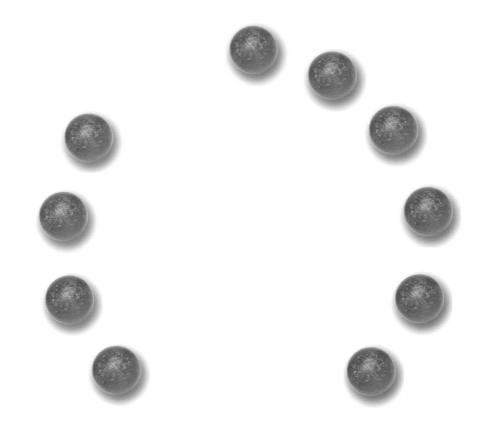

$$4 + 6 = ?$$

What if you started with 4 balls and added 6 more?

Would you still have 10 balls?

Start at 4 and count on 6 times.

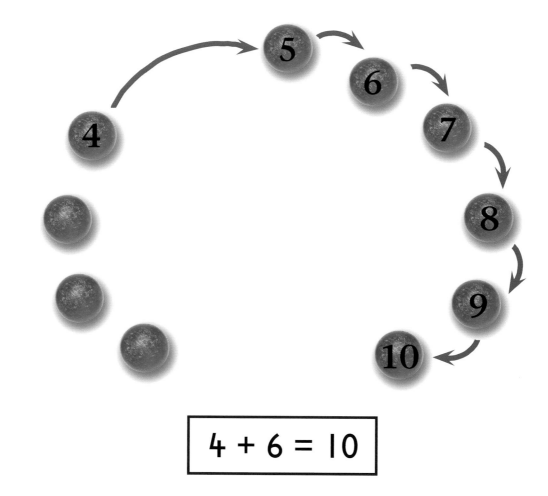

$$4 + 6 = 10$$

The total number of balls is the same.

You can start with 6 balls and add 4.

Or you can start with 4 balls and add 6.

Either way, they combine to make the same number.

Practising adding

Adding is like putting things in a bag.

You can add things in any order.

You get the same number in the end.

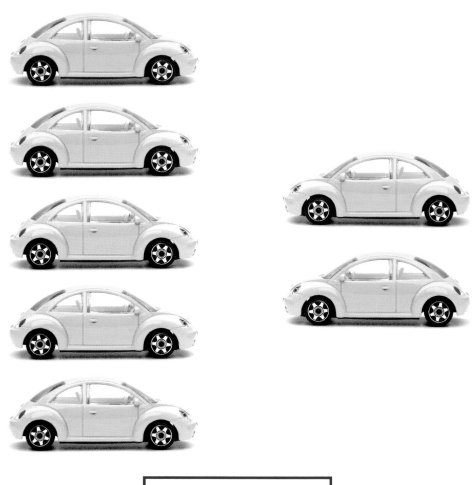

$$5 + 2 = 7$$

Practise adding your own toys.

Adding becomes easier the more you practise!

Quiz

You have 6 shells.

Someone gives you 3 more.

Can you count on to find out how many shells you have now?

0 1 2 3 4 5 6 7 8 9 10

The plus sign

| + | You use this sign to show that you are adding numbers. |

$$3 + 2$$

When you add 3 and 2, you get 5.

| = | You use the equals sign to show what 3 plus 2 is equal to. |

$$3 + 2 = 5$$

Index

Answer to the quiz on page 22
You have 9 shells now.

Note to parents and teachers
Reading non-fiction texts for information is an important part of a child's literacy development. Readers can be encouraged to ask simple questions and then use the text to find the answers. Most chapters in this book begin with a question. Read the questions together. Look at the pictures. Talk about what the answer might be. Then read the text to find out if your predictions were correct. To develop readers' enquiry skills, encourage them to think of other questions they might ask about the topic. Discuss where you could find the answers. Assist children in using the contents page, picture glossary and index to practise research skills and new vocabulary.

Titles in the **Simple Maths** series include:

Hardback 1 4062 0390 4
978 1 4062 0390 5

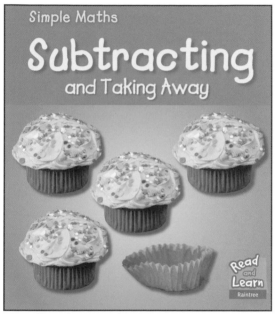

Hardback 1 4062 0391 2
978 1 4062 0391 2

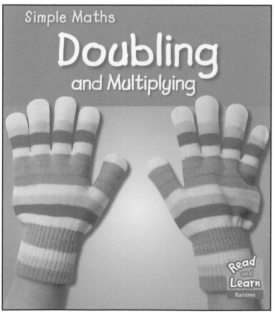

Hardback 1 4062 0392 0
978 1 4062 0392 9

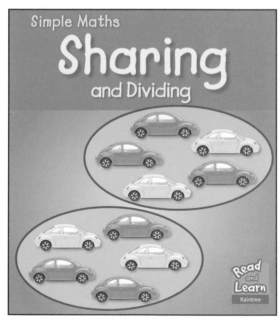

Hardback 1 4062 0393 9
978 1 4062 0393 6

Find out more about the other titles in this series on our website www.raintreepublishers.co.uk